I remember one of your first visits after I moved to NYC, you mentioned while passing some skyscrapers how you loved art deco. Some time it took, but thank to Andrew I've found just how much

❤ Addison Dec '22

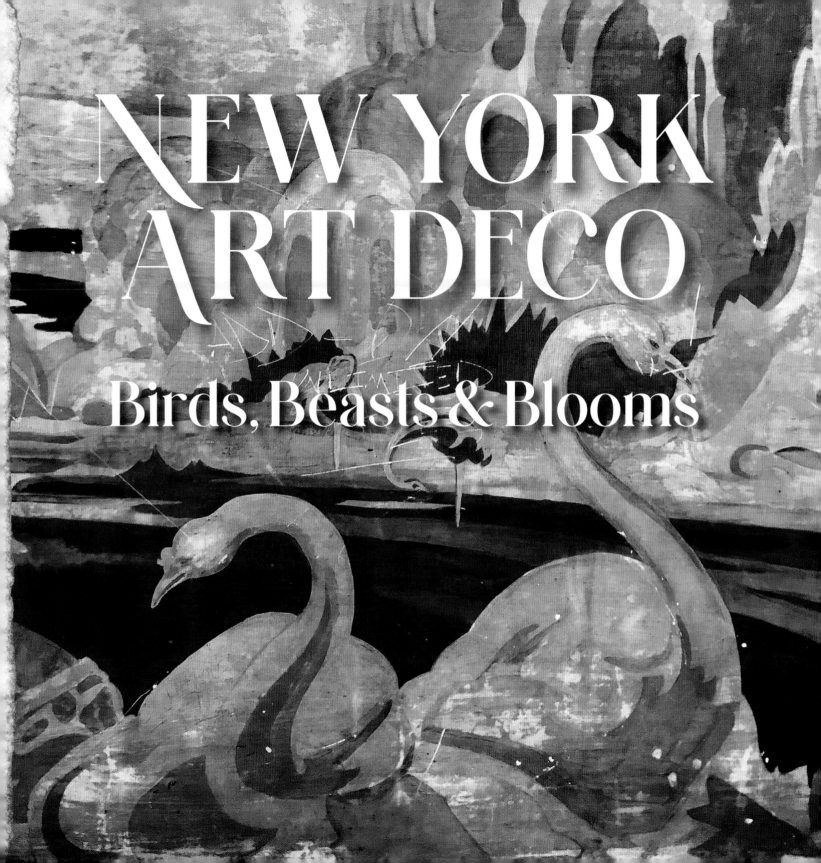

NEW YORK ART DECO

Birds, Beasts & Blooms

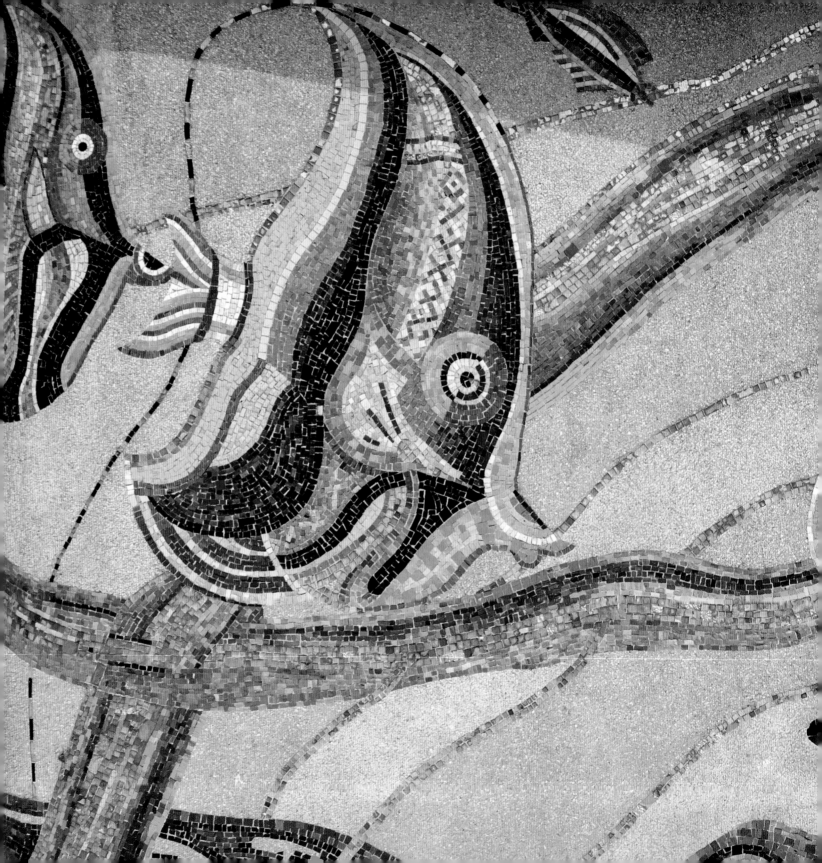

NEW YORK ART DECO

Birds, Beasts & Blooms

Photography by **ANDREW GARN**

Introduction by **ERIC P. NASH**

ENJOY
NYC!
-ERIC

To Mike!

A

RIZZOLI
NEW YORK

New York · Paris · London · Milan

First published in the United States of America in 2022 by

RIZZOLI INTERNATIONAL PUBLICATIONS, INC.

300 Park Avenue South, New York, NY 10010

www.rizzoliusa.com

© 2022 Rizzoli International Publications, Inc.

Text © 2022 Eric P. Nash

Photography © 2022 Andrew Garn

Publisher: Charles Miers

Editor: Douglas Curran

Production Manager: Kaija Markoe

Managing Editor: Lynn Scrabis

Proofreader: Sarah Stump

Designed by Aldo Sampieri

Printed and bound in China

2022 2023 2024 2025 2026 / 10 9 8 7 6 5 4 3 2 1

ISBN-13: 978-0-8478-7204-6

Library of Congress Control Number: 2022934527

Page 1: Lobby mural at 1150 Grand Concourse, Bronx (see page 174)

Pages 2–3: Decorative tile at entry to 1150 Grand Concourse, Bronx

Page 4: Bas-relief metalwork at Rockefeller Center (see page 178)

Visit us online:

Facebook.com/RizzoliNewYork

Twitter: @Rizzoli_Books

Instagram.com/RizzoliBooks

Pinterest.com/RizzoliBooks

Youtube.com/user/RizzoliNY

Issuu.com/Rizzoli

CONTENTS

A sharp-winged, gilded vulture represents the intermediary between the realms of life and death in Egyptian mythology.
Detail from exterior facade of the Pythian, 135 West 70th Street (see page 65)

INTRODUCTION
A Streamlined History of Art Deco
by Eric P. Nash

And to me also, who appreciates life, the butterflies, and soap bubbles, and
whatever is like them amongst us, seem to enjoy happiness.

—Friedrich Nietzsche, *Thus Spake Zarathustra*

The Long and Winding Road to Art Deco

Art Deco in New York is forever associated with the fizzy energy of the Jazz Age—flappers, speakeasies, the gleaming tiara of the Chrysler Building—everything that was new and swellegant about the second decade of the twentieth century, but its stylistic roots go deeper. One critic noted that Deco's influences range from the "ancient past to the distant future." Deco is easy to recognize, but as difficult to pin down as a blob of mercury.

Deco was a wild party after the mechanized carnage of the Great War and the ravages of the Spanish Flu, which ultimately killed more people worldwide. American and French victors relished making whoopie in newfound peace and precious, fleeting life itself. Americans called the years from 1923 to 1929 the "Coolidge Prosperity," after our thirtieth president, Calvin "Cool Cal" Coolidge.

Art movements evolve from one another, so preceding styles are critical to understanding Art Deco. The new style was an overlay, rather than a complete replacement, of its botanically based predecessor, Art Nouveau. The artist most associated in the popular mind with Art Nouveau is Alphonse Mucha, who created blush-toned, intricately detailed posters with his mastery of the delicate art of limestone lithography, which required exacting tinctures of four-color oils and water. Nouveau served as a means of escapism into an opium-induced fairyland, in response to an era of soot-belching locomotives.

Born in Czechoslovakia, Mucha had a brief, brilliant career in the late nineteenth century as the toast of tout Paris. Clients lined up around the block to order his posters, which were ubiquitous on kiosks and city walls. Previously, advertising bills were in monotonous black and white typeface. For the first time, *tout le monde* was introduced to glorious color. Strangely, Mucha never considered his work to be Art Nouveau, but saw it as an extension of Czech folk art.

Incidentally, Mucha enjoyed a tremendous resurgence in acid rock posters of the mid-1960s by West Coast artists Stanley Mouse, Victor Moscoso, and others, which are now prized collectors' items in their own right. These psychedelic poster-makers swiped Mucha's muses, like the Job cigarette girl, "noodle style," hair and all, even as it was called back in the 1890s. They amped up their palettes to eleven to achieve eyeball-vibrating, saturated colors meant to mimic an LSD experience. Acid rock posters with near-unintelligible typefaces were made for everybody from Janis Joplin and Jefferson Airplane, to the Grateful Dead.

A lesser-known painter and lithograph poster artist, Jules Chéret, was considered to be the "father of the modern poster," and by many critics a superior artist than Mucha, for his use of bold primary reds and yellows, free line in depicting dancehall mademoiselles, and creative lettering. Nevertheless, Chéret was cast in Mucha's shadow, except among the cognoscenti, where his first editions command equally dizzying heights at auction.

Another major Parisian Art Nouveau designer and architect was Hector Guimard, designer of the renowned, asparagus-green-painted, cast-iron and milky glass entryways to the Paris Métro stations (1898–1901), whose muted amber lights droop at nighttime like the pedicels of some stalk-eyed creature from an absinthe dream.

The public rightly was leery of the machine as an engine of destruction. Art Deco served to palliate fear of the machine by celebrating its glory in a cleaner, leaner iconography: powerful locomotives, luxury liners, squadrons of airplanes flying in formation, and that *dernier crí* in transatlantic travel, the zeppelin.

For the first time, our book, *New York Art Deco: Birds, Beasts & Blooms*, focuses on a softer, gentler side of Deco, in depictions of nature-based imagery, as a means of ingratiating the public to the Machine Age.

Americans have a deep and abiding reverence for nature. There is a long painterly and literary tradition of American naturalism, from Hudson River School landscape painters like Frederic Church and Thomas Cole in the 1830s; the now nearly obscure but hugely influential horticulturalist and author Andrew Jackson Davis, known as the "Apostle of Taste" for middle class landscaping in the decades before the Civil War; New England Transcendentalists Ralph Waldo Emerson, who published his philosophy in a seminal book, *Nature*, in 1836, and Henry David Thoreau, who wrote *Walden* in 1865, an idyll from the bloody Civil War; genius landscape architects Frederick

Law Olmsted and Calvin Vaux, who created the emerald paradises of Central Park and Brooklyn's Prospect Park; and Ansel Adams in the relatively new medium of photography.

It's only natural then, so to speak, that Deco designers used flora and fauna to introduce Deco into the contemporary public consciousness. Organic Deco, drawn from nature, derives from as many sources as Art Deco itself, a mélange of futuristic motifs combined with ancient styles—Mayan, Aztec, Egyptian, Mesopotamian, Sumerian, Babylonian—you name it; sometimes all at once, like in the fever dream of the Pythian Temple (1927) on New York's Upper West Side, designed by Barnum-esque theater architect Thomas W. Lamb, who pulled out all the stops.

Two-dimensional bands of chevrons and stripes were adopted to make the viewer scan designs in rapid horizontals, heightening the sensation of speed, motion, and forward progress. Colorful materials like patinated bronze, nickel, polychromatic terracotta (a decorative, colorful form of glazed clay tile—terracotta literally means "baked earth"), and gilded limestone added to the garden of delights of urban architecture.

Birds, beasts, and blooms are cheerful, surprising, and easy to recognize, if you know where to look. They serve to remind city dwellers of more pleasant things than the burning tarmac beneath our feet in summer or the cruelty of winter, known by the aptronym "the hawk" in old jazz lingo.

Deco was also a populist response to revolutions that rocked the arts in the early twentieth century, changing the way we perceive the world. Japonisme, the flat, two-dimensional Ukiyo-e prints from Japan, were eagerly collected by Parisian artists, as well as a young American architect named Frank Lloyd Wright, who sometimes staved off his debtors by selling a choice piece or two. Other contemporaneous movements that shaped a new Weltanschauung were Fauvism's wild palette; multifaceted Cubism that fragmented our point of view; the jarring angularity of German Expressionism; bellicose Italian Futurism that attempted to capture motion on canvas and in sculpture; the oneiric juxtapositions of Surrealism; the bright primaries and severe geometry of De Stijl in the Netherlands; the inventive iconoclasm of Russian Constructivism; and the riotous, Oriental-inspired patterns of costumes and sets for the Diaghilev's Ballet Russes designed by Picasso, Matisse, Coco Chanel, and Paul Poiret.

For us nature lovers, Art Deco, which dates as far back as 1907, presents a welcome menagerie of elephants; ungulates from gangly giraffes to springboks and *biches*; a fully stocked aviary of storks, geese, cranes, pelicans, uncountable owls, and eagles; as well as an ichthyologist's wet dream of octopuses, mollusks, seaweed, flounder, dangling invertebrate jellyfish, even psychedelic angelfish, like something out of *Yellow Submarine*.

Identifying Deco

The term Art Deco was never used in its day. Styles were interchangeably referred to as Modern, Modernistic, or Art Modern; confusing today, because the labels now have different connotations. The umbrella term Art Deco was coined by the British art historian Bevis Hillier in 1968 in his slim but landmark survey, *Art Deco of the 20s and 30s*, the first book to examine the style as a whole. Hillier used the name as an anglicized shorthand for the celebrated *Exposition internationale des artes décoratifs et industriels modernes* held in Paris in 1925. The succinct phrase stuck, unlike other duds including *Style Maxims* (for the celebrated fin-de-siècle Parisian restaurant, and the gastronomically unappealing *Bandwurmstil* ("tapeworm style" in German). There probably wouldn't be a craze today for "Tapeworm Style."

Curiously, Hillier, despite his giant steps, overlooked the contribution of the Americas to Deco, other than to acknowledge the influence of Southwestern Native American and Mayan motifs. He recanted in his subsequent book, *The World of Art Deco*, which accompanied the first large, modern-day Deco exhibition at the Minneapolis Institute of Arts in 1971:

I can only claim in mitigation that mine was the first book in English on the subject. Looking back, I ask: how could I have possibly written on Art Deco with not a single mention of Radio City Music Hall (which now seems to me *the* Art Deco shrine) or the Chanin Building and Chrysler Building, New York.

Transplated from France, Art Deco captured the global imagination as a symbol of all that was chic and contemporary, from a skyscraper-themed, gentleman's silk under-kimono in Tokyo, to aspiring outposts of empire, like Havana, Mumbai, Shanghai, La Condessa (a delightful neighborhood of brightly painted Deco apartment buildings and violet-colored jacaranda trees in Mexico City), and in the antipodes in Melbourne and Sydney, Australia, and Napier, New Zealand, which has the largest concentration of Art Deco buildings in the world—an entire city leveled by an earthquake in 1931 and rebuilt in a Deco style incorporating indigenous Maori motifs.

Metalwork detail from the Madison Belmont Building, 181 Madison Avenue (see page 36)

The Dawn of Deco in America

Unlike Nouveau, Deco caught on like kindling, then like wildfire in the American imagination. Nouveau was residential, boutique-oriented, whimsical. Americans had no time for whimsy; they were too busy building skyscrapers and making money.

Deco first arrived on America's shores not in the form of building ornamentation, but rather through the front door, so to speak, in home furnishings promoted by department stores like Macy's and John Wanamaker. In combination with the Metropolitan Museum of Art, Macy's put on a series of exhibitions called the *Exposition of Art in Trade* in 1927. It was a clever gambit, because the store became associated with the prestige and imprimatur of the museum, at the same popularizing the style to the public. The next year, a quarter of a million people came to see Macy's international exposition *Art in Industry*, which displayed more than five thousand modern art objects by three hundred exhibitors from six countries.

A contemporary critic wrote that department stores had become "a living museum of the industrial and decorative arts, in which the ideas of artist-designers incorporated in furniture, textiles, ceramics, etcetera, are, through mass production, made available to the masses."

Department store owners found that Americans were eager to buy modernistic design, as long as the prices were in line with more traditional furniture. One luxe table was even upholstered in dolphin skin (!). An entire Parisian room has been transported to the Brooklyn Museum—the Weil-Worgelt Study of 1930, with its muted tobacco colors of palisander and olivewood veneer, a lacquer screen, and an etched-glass bar. The lounge chairs are surprisingly elfin, perfect for notoriously low-ceilinged New York apartments.

The style's prestige was evident in major municipal buildings like the rocket-shaped Nebraska State Capitol (Bertram Grosvenor Goodhue, 1920) that dominates the plains of the Cornhusker State; the classic Deco massing of Los Angeles City Hall (Austin, Parkinson & Martin, 1928), familiar to TV-watchers from *Dragnet*, *CHiPs*, and nearly every other cop show set in Southern California (earthquake-prone Los Angeles is not renowned for its tall buildings); and the mountain-like Buffalo City Hall (Dietel, Wade & Jones, 1932).

Deco's mass popularity is evident everywhere, from local cinemas, to gas stations, and luncheonettes. The style was the bee's knees on Hollywood musical sets of many Fred Astaire and Ginger Rogers movies and Busby Berkeley's automaton-like extravaganzas of synchronized swimmers and tap-dancers, in films like *Footlight Parade* (1933)

Even though the United States was in the depths of a Great Depression, it was still one of the few nations wealthy enough to produce and distribute culturally influential flicks worldwide, making the Manhattan penthouse synonymous with sophistication and cosmopolitanism.

In the marketplace, suddenly *tout le monde* had access to modern design on a budget, in everything from butterscotch-colored Bakelite radio sets to inexpensive yet chic baubles and bangles.

The syncopated Manhattan skyline, the cynosure of Art Deco, was due to something as mundane as a change in a civic zoning code. After the turn of the twentieth century, New York office buildings, notably Ernest R. Graham's Equitable Building of 1915 (which still stands on Lower Broadway), were burgeoning to unreasonable proportions.

The Equitable packed in an astonishing 1.2 million square feet of office space—thirty times the size of its footprint—into forty-one stories that took up an entire block and cast a shadow six times its height, causing nearby real estate values to plummet. Civic leaders, under pressure from commercial landowners, decided that something had to done to restore the circulation of light and air to the streets.

They came up with the so-called setback Zoning Code of 1916, which required that the upper stories of a building be stepped back according to a certain formula from the line where the building touched the sidewalk. The results were as revolutionary as they were unexpected. Architects felt they had a new building typology to work with in the setback skyscraper that required a new, modernistic design. Chance met opportunity—the sleek Deco look from the Paris exposition was adapted to the tall New York building, and the classic "wedding cake" Deco skyscraper was born.

A paradox of Deco was that in order to escape the shackles of the Neoclassical and Beaux-Arts past that had held a grip on architecture for centuries, designers felt a need to seek evermore *recherché* sources for inspiration, including Babylonian, Assyrian, the "Nile Style," or all three together (why not?), like the eclectic (to put it mildly) Pythian Temple on West 70th Street, with winged lions, chimeras, seated pharaohs, and square-bearded Sumerians that could have been lifted straight from a historically challenged set designer's plans for a D. W. Griffith or Cecil B. DeMille movie.

A veritable "Murderers' Row" of Deco glories followed in rapid succession—the Chanin Building (Sloan & Robertson, 1928), with its bronze frieze depicting evolution by untouted but omnipresent architectural sculptor René Paul Chambellan; William Van Alen's extraordinary cadmium-nickel crowned Chrysler Building of 1930 (the idiosyncratic architect's only major commission, besides various Childs restaurants, a popular chain of the time); culminating in the Empire State Building (Shreve, Lamb & Harmon, 1931), the world's tallest building of the time at 102 stories.

The urbane complex of Rockefeller Center (1931–1939), which took nearly a full decade to complete, features a decorative program replete with a menagerie of animals and a gardens of luxuriant, herbal motifs by Deco masters Lee Lawrie, Chambellan, and Paul Manship, the most celebrated and prosperous architectural sculptor of his time.

The decorative scheme was so ambitious, the Rockefellers even hired a consulting philosopher, Hartley Burr Alexander of Scripps University, to devise a theme for it: "Homo Fabor—Man the Builder," later changed to "The March of Civilization"—capitalism's answer to the rise of Bolshevism and the Fascist threat.

Art Deco is remarkable in that a single material fragment of it, like a flapper's hoydenish bobbed hairstyle, cloche hat, nifty silk shift with a plunging neckline, long loop of artificial pearls, and slender cigarette holder, reveals the louche insouciance, fun, frivolity, and lightheartedness with which the culture embraced the moment, its dedication to hedonism, like the evanescent essence of a soap bubble of which Nietzsche spake.

Nature has always had a soothing effect on human beings, reminding us that we, too, belong to the earth, and are its rightful stewards and conservators. The Japanese, of course, have a term for the restorative sensation of nature: *shin-rikyu*, literally "forest bathing." It is no surprise that people hurtling headlong into the twentieth and twenty-first centuries resort to natural imagery to ease the transition. Contemporary architects, like wunderkind Bjarke Ingels, have incorporated leafy bowers into their work, as seen on the Spiral at Hudson Yards.

Birds, beasts, and blooms have been the subject of decorative art as old as Ishtar; Art Deco in New York is no different.

opposite: Bull's head ornament in pediment at 20 Exchange Place (see page 122)

pages 18–19: Bas-relief metalwork at Rockefeller Center (see page 178)

HERMAN LEE MEADER, ARCHITECT

Built in 1913, the commercial and office building at 154 West 14th Street is a phenomenal early transition from Art Nouveau and Neoclassical design to Art Deco. The terracotta colors are muddier than the later brilliance of Deco. Dark green fronds flank a polyhedral object, surmounted by a blue meandros, a continuous line in a repeating pattern taken from Greek antiquity. The facade (above) is a liberal mix of motifs—a yellow-winged disk representing the sun god Horus in Egyptian mythology, a blue Greek meandros named for the winding Meander River in Turkey (from which me derive the word "meander"), pentahedrons set in disks, and flanking green fronds. Spaghetti-like intertwining white lotus stems against a mustard background with azure accents (opposite, top left) are a transitional pattern from Art Nouveau to Art Deco. The white petals of an anthemion or palmetto (opposite, top right), a classical Greek motif, stand out against mustard-colored panels, surmounting a repeating green frond pattern.

243 Riverside Drive · 1914

CLIFF DWELLING, HERMAN LEE MEADER

Cliff Dwelling, designed by Herman Lee Meader in 1914, offers an early expression of some familiar
Art Deco motifs, including Mayan, Aztec, and American Western–inspired imagery, as seen on this frieze of the building's facade.

FRIENDS HOUSE (ORIGINALLY B. W. MAYER BUILDING)
HERMAN LEE MEADER, ARCHITECT
An apparently Mayan-inspired treasure on East 25th Street, Friends House originally served as offices, then for many years as a trade school. In 1994 the Quakers purchased the building and restored it to its present, somewhat mysterious glory.

135 West 36ᵗʰ Street · 1922

FASHION TOWER
EMERY ROTH, ARCHITECT
Exuberantly decorative, Fashion Tower was designed by Emery Roth. Best known for apartment houses and other
residential work, Roth's tower in the Garment District of Manhattan bridges the gap between the outgoing Art Nouveau style and
the emerging Art Deco movement, offering on this facade elements of both styles, such as the peacock—a popular Art Nouveau
motif—as well as elaborate angular embellishments more indicative of Deco.

110 East 42ⁿᵈ Street · 1923

BOWERY SAVINGS BANK BUILDING
YORK & SAWYER, ARCHITECTS
This masterful piece of architecture from York & Sawyer is often considered to be Italian Romanesque Revival in stye, with its towering round arches and brickwork, but an argument can be made for its Art Deco leanings. Here, as ornament, we see pelicans, eagles, griffins, various beasts, turbaned figures, and holy men, all hinting of the exotic—one of the great hallmarks of the Art Deco style.

16 Park Avenue · 1924

FRED F. FRENCH, ARCHITECT

The Fred F. French Building, headquarters for the eponymous developer who built Tudor City, was designed by the prominent Art Deco firm of Sloan & Robertson, featuring mythical beasts and chimeras inspired by ancient Assyrian figures (above). In Babylonian mythology, Hermes was the twin snake god (opposite, top), both male and female, the most potent fertility symbol in the animal kingdom. The modern medical caduceus is a descendant of Hermes, with two snakes, symbols of immortality merged with the Rod of Asclepius, the Greek god of healing. Twin oxen merge in a single head with horns (opposite, bottom). Oxen were important in Assyrian warfare as draft animals and for food.

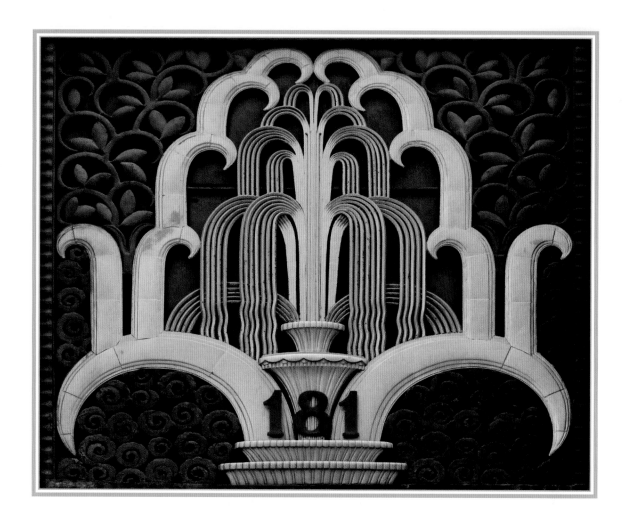

MADISON BELMONT BUILDING
WARREN & WETMORE, ARCHITECTS
EDGAR BRANDT, METALWORK

Built in 1925 by Warren & Wetmore, the Madison Belmont Building represents the firm's transition from Beaux-Arts to Art Deco, with spectacular patinated iron and bronze showroom frames, grilles, and gates and gilded bronze entrance doors by the Frenchman Edgar Brandt, who designed the wrought iron entrance gates of the 1925 Paris exposition, and was considered the world's "greatest exponent of Art Deco metalwork." This "frozen fountain" motif by Brandt in gilded bronze (above), set against a floral iron background, became typical in Deco design, representing the freshness and vitality of the new decorative art, as well as reflecting the setback skyscraper style. Brandt combined Egyptian, Greek, and Pompeiian motifs, like these gilded bronze Egyptian lilies bearing papyrus bundles (opposite, top right), from which the earliest form of paper was derived.

STANDPIPE
THROUGHOUT
BUILDING

101 East 161st Street, Bronx · 1925

Twin horseheads, chevrons, and rope columns adorn the cornice of this apartment building on the Grand Concourse in the Bronx. The concourse itself, modeled after the Champs-Élysées but much larger, was built by French-born engineer Louis Aloys Riss between 1894 and 1909. By the mid-1930s more than three hundred Deco and Streamline Moderne apartment buildings lined its borders.

110 West Street · 1927

THE VERIZON BUILDING (FORMERLY THE NEW YORK TELEPHONE COMPANY BUILDING)
RALPH WALKER, ARCHITECT

The decorative program of the former New York Telephone Building on West Street was designed by ornamental sculptors
Ulysses Ricci and John De Cesare in cast stone, less costly than limestone—using the aid of machines when possible—features birds,
beasts, and flowers. Within (following pages), jungle beasts, lianas, and pendulous fruit are rendered in a Deco style that was a radical
departure from the Neoclassical. In a metal frieze above the entrance canopy, fish, dolphins, and starfish romp in the waves,
perhaps in celebration of the first transatlantic telephone call, which took place in 1927.

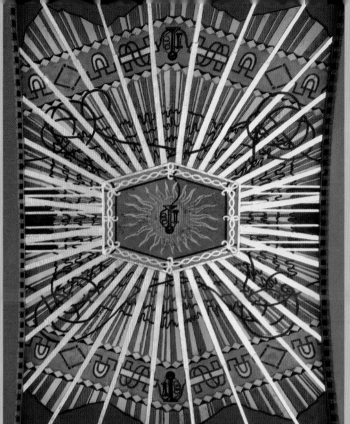

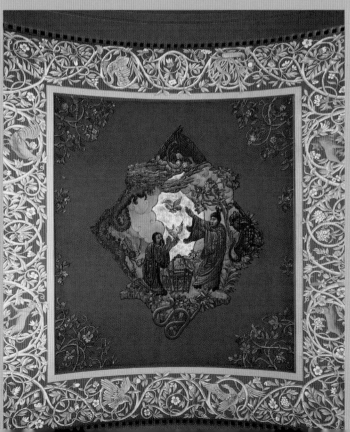

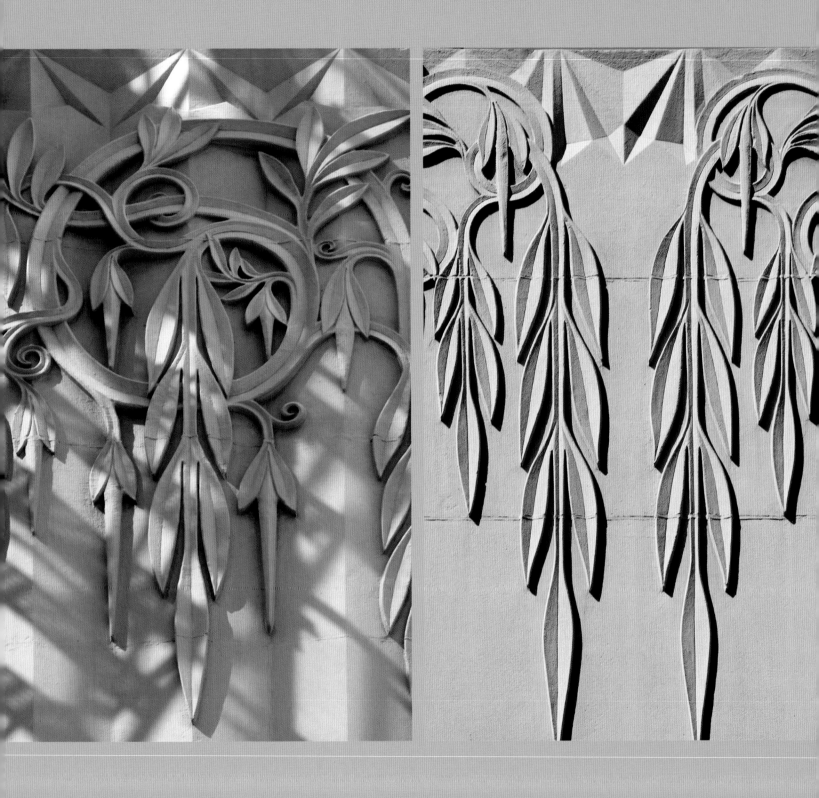

STELLA TOWER
RALPH WALKER, ARCHITECT
Stylized plant forms, with vines, flowers, and fruit, adorn the exterior facade and entry frieze at the Stella Tower,
a former Bell Telephone building and one of dozens throughout the city designed by Ralph Walker of Voorhees, Gmelin &
Walker. Walker admired the ornamentation of Louis Sullivan, whose influence is in evidence here.

274 Madison Avenue · 1927

ALEXANDER WILSON BUILDING
SLOAN & ROBERTSON, ARCHITECTS

Entryway ornament at the Alexander Wilson Building by architects Sloan & Robertson, best known for their design of the Chanin and Graybar buildings. Initially made for retail purposes, the building has been converted over the years to creative office space. Decorative elements include sinuous grape vines and crowned peacocks.

48

FRED F. FRENCH BUILDING
SLOAN & ROBERTSON, ARCHITECTS

The Fred F. French Building, headquarters for the eponymous developer who built Tudor City, was designed by the prominent Art Deco firm of Sloan & Robertson, featuring mythical beasts and chimeras inspired by ancient Assyrian figures. The Assyrian-themed lobby (opposite and pages 54–57) features one of the most elaborate Art Deco programs in the city. Griffins top a gilded lunette of horses and riders, hounds, and palm trees. The legendary griffin (pages 52–53) bears the head, wings, and talons of an eagle with the body of lion. The eagle is the king of birds, and the lion the king of beasts, so the griffin bears the regal manner of both. The bronze mail chute (above) boasts a spread-winged eagle, representing the Federal government, emanating sunrays, and paired griffins. The lobby's highlight is a spectacular, suspended, foliated Deco lamp in frosted white glass and bronze (opposite). Top that!

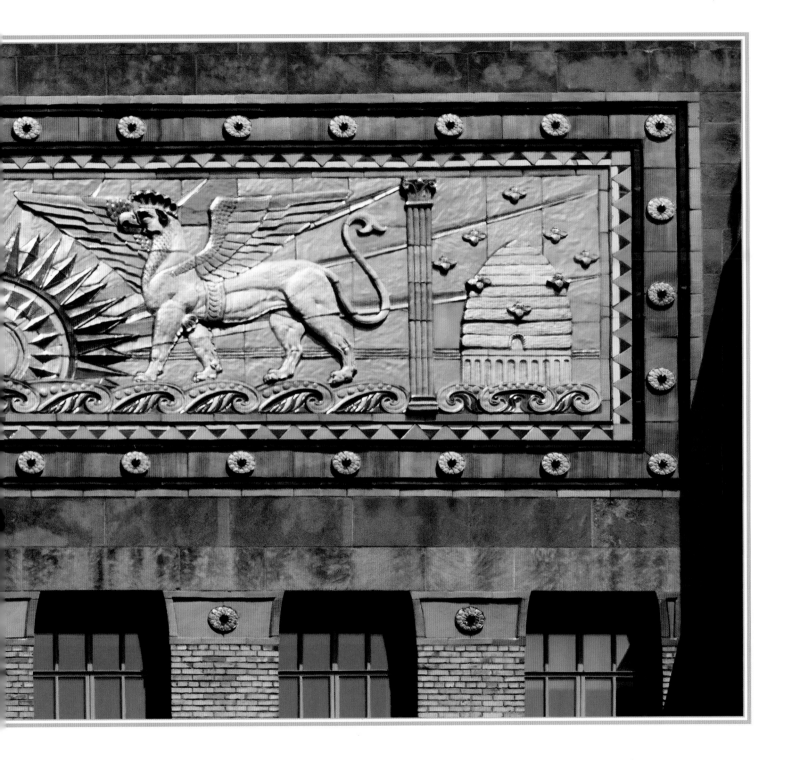

53

125 East 50th Street · 1927

THE BENJAMIN
EMERY ROTH, ARCHITECT

Traditionally, pelicans (opposite) are symbols of motherly love and self-sacrifice, based on the myth that they pierce their own breasts with their beaks to provide life-giving blood to their brood. While the Deco owl (above) radiates wisdom at the Benjamin Hotel, designed by Emery Roth.

GRAYBAR BUILDING
SLOAN & ROBERTSON, ARCHITECTS
The Graybar Building, an early, large Deco office building next to Grand Central Terminal, features winged "guardians,"
Deco and Renaissance Revival style lion's heads that hold mooring cables, and a strange, finned sea creature—a myriad of
references to the maritime trade of a great port city. Deco architects often like to have fun with the ornamental schemes of
their buildings. Deco-esque rats (following pages, right) are prevented by baffles from entering the moorings lines that
suspend a canopy of the Graybar Building, a tribute to New York's maritime history. The rosettes are cleverly composed of the heads
of rats who have already made it aboard. The original rat sculptures were lost or stolen, and have been replaced by later replicas.

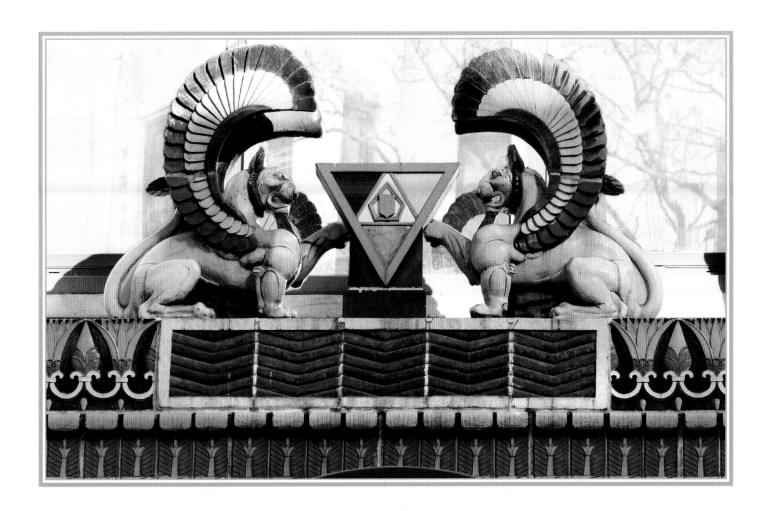

THE PYTHIAN (FORMERLY PYTHIAN TEMPLE)
THOMAS W. LAMB, ARCHITECT

This farrago of Nilotic, Assyrian, Sumerian, Babylonian, and Greek symbols on the former Pythian Temple, one of the city's more exotic Deco facades, was designed by master movie palace architect Thomas W. Lamb in the so-called Egyptian Revival style. An orange sun disk (following page, bottom), flanked by wings with blue and russet feathers, symbolizes the Egyptian sun god, Ra. Cobras, a sign of royalty, are found on pharaohs' headdresses while a vulture greets a pharaonic gilded cobra bearing the lamp of wisdom on its head (following pages, right), next to an Ankh cross, a symbol of eternal life. Just who were these Knights of Pythias?. The Knights of Pythias are a fraternal, charitable organization with a penchant for mystic symbols, who were compelled to sell the building to Decca Records. Bill Haley and his Comets made rock 'n roll history cutting their smash single "Rock Around the Clock" at Decca's recording studio here in 1954.

261 Fifth Avenue · 1928

ELY JACQUES KAHN, ARCHITECT

The vibrant Jazz-Age Deco structure at 261 Fifth Avenue is a unlike any other in the city. Designed by Ely Jacques Kahn,
the twenty-six-story multi-purpose building, with its wonderfully preserved lobby, original lighting, and other
features (above), employs geometric bands and vivid terracotta on its exterior facade.

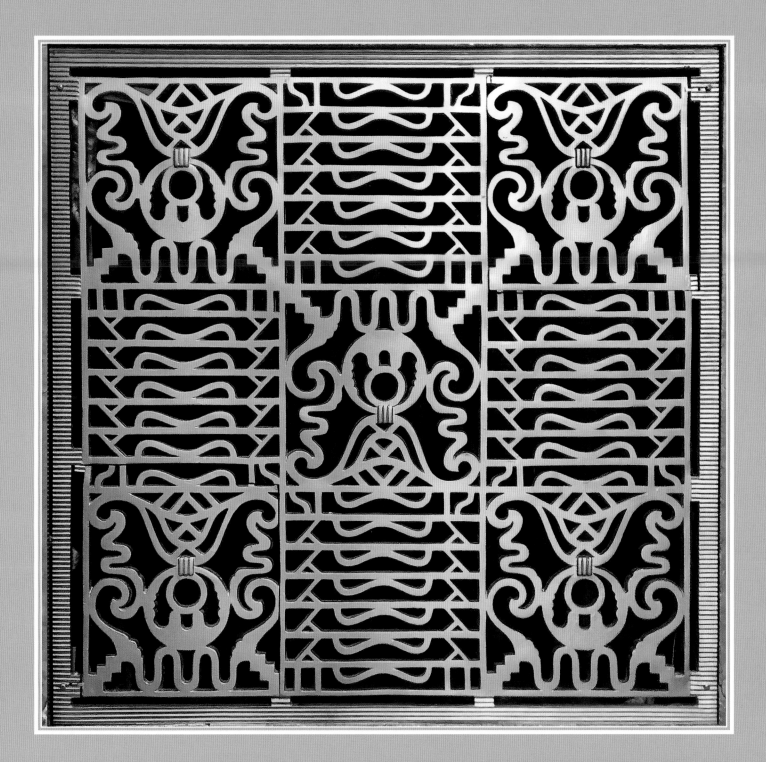

3 East 84th Street · 1928

RAYMOND HOOD AND JOHN MEAD HOWELLS, ARCHITECTS

Raymond Hood and John Mead Howells, well known for their stunning early Deco skyscraper,
the American Radiator Building, designed this apartment house on New York's Upper East Side,
a gem of simple yet rich ornamentation, as epitomized here in metalwork done in vegetal motifs.

102 East 22nd Street · 1928

GRAMERCY ARMS
SUGARMAN & BURGER, ARCHITECTS
One block from storied Gramercy Park, the ten-story Gramercy Arms, at 102 East 22nd Street
offers a subdued Deco glamour in brick and terracotta.

304 East 44th Street · 1928

BEAUX ARTS INSTITUTE OF DESIGN
FREDERIC C. HIRONS, ARCHITECT

Despite its name, the Beaux Arts Institute, a former school of art and architecture in Turtle Bay, was completed in a Deco style in 1930, in a competition won by British architect Frederic C. Hirons, who beat notable architects such as Raymond Hood, William Van Alen, and Arthur Loomis Harmon. Receding terracotta pilaster capitals with circular daisies, ochre-colored windmill petals, and twisted blue stems flank crisply geometric green ferns. Founded by New York University in 1916, the Beaux Arts Institute of Design later moved into this more spacious building at 304 East 44th Street in 1930. The building is now residential in quiet Turtle Bay.

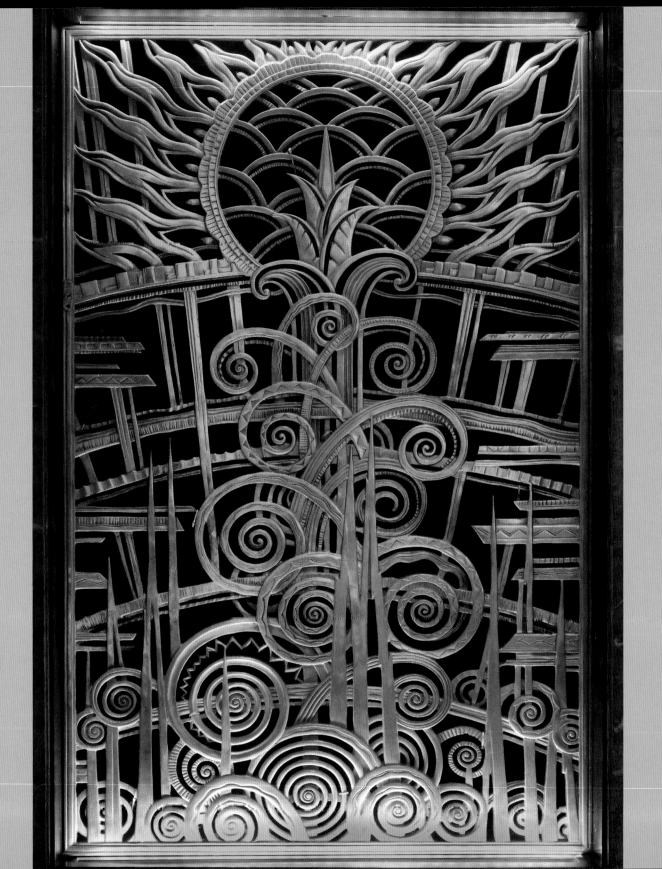

CHANIN BUILDING
SLOAN & ROBERTSON, ARCHITECTS
JACQUES DELAMARRE, LOBBY DESIGN • RENÉ CHAMBELLAN, SCULPTOR

The lobby and exterior frieze of the Chanin Building, in the shadow of the showier Chrysler Building, are the acme of sculptor René Paul Chambellan's work, along with the limestone grille on the exterior of the Daily News Building and the fountains of Rockefeller Center. A gilded bronze radiator grille with curling fronds, a central blossom, and radiating leaves reveals his attention to detail (opposite). The astonishing bronze frieze just above street level was executed by Chambellan with architectural sculptor Jaques L. Delamarre Sr., best known for his decorative programs of the Art Deco classics the Century and Majestic apartment buildings on Central Park West. The theme of the French Modern Classical frieze (above and following pages, right) is evolution from sea life beginning with primitive amoeba, culminating in flight, with images of geese flapping their wings, an emblem of the soaring ambitions of the skyscraper itself.

BEEKMAN TOWER (PANHELLENIC TOWER)
JOHN MEAD HOWELLS, ARCHITECT
This twenty-six story Art Deco skyscraper was built for the Panhellenic Association's New York chapter as a club and hotel for women in sororities, and later was converted to a general hotel and then apartments. Its roseate sandstone sculptural ornamentation was designed by René Paul Chambellan (following pages).

681 Eighth Avenue · 1928

(FORMERLY STATE BANK AND TRUST COMPANY BUILDING)
DENNISON & HIRONS, ARCHITECTS

A prominently sited polychromatic terracotta panel at the corner of Eighth Avenue and West 43rd Street for the former State Bank and Trust Company Building displays Chambellan's French Classical Modern stye, with low-relief designs of interlacing curled ferns and flowers. His widely reproduced (and knocked off) patterns, a Deco staple, can be found on apartment and office buildings, and humble savings bank branches in media including plain and polychrome terracotta, carved limestone, and plaster. A terracotta pilaster capital (opposite) features paired, cream-colored ferns, flanking a blooming light-yellow lotus flower and matched viridian fronds.

87

METROPOLITAN LIFE NORTH BUILDING
CORBETT & WAID, ARCHITECTS
Architects Harvey Wiley Corbett and D. Everett Waid originally schemed to build a mountainous, telescoping tower of eighty to one hundred stories on the northwest corner of Madison Square Garden, but the developers went bust, and the stump remained a twenty-eight-story monument to the Depression, the reason why the entrances are so out of scale. A detail of the gates in the limestone base shows a highly styled Renaissance Revival overlay on vaguely Deco vegetal metal forms (opposite). Corbett was a visionary who dreamed that a tower purely of glass and metal would top the base.

7 Gracie Square · 1929

GEORGE B. POST AND SONS, ARCHITECTS
EDGAR BRANDT, DECORATIVE IRONWORK

Magnificent metalwork doors by French designer Edgar Brandt adorn 7 Gracie Square, an Art Deco apartment house just off East End Avenue by Carl Schurz Park. A wrought iron double door features a fantasia of foliate tracery patterns. Brandt pioneered the use of industrial methods in decorative ironwork, including torch welding and power hammers. Brandt's foliated and floral design for this door and pediment with antelopes in bas-relief has the feel of bronze and terracotta work by the much-copied American architectural sculptor René Paul Chambellan, whose distinctive style has been alternately described as Deco and French Classical Modern.

The facade of 367 East 149th Street in the Bronx is notable for
its array of sea life, including grouper, amoebae, and sea plants, flanked by
American eagles, which recall their proud cousins at the nearby Bronx County Courthouse.

444 Central Park West · 1929

BOAK & PARIS, ARCHITECTS

This building at 444 Central Park West was designed by Emery Roth alumni Russell Boak and Hyman Paris in 1929. Its facade, of brick and terracotta, is enlivened by ornamentation that includes various floral and avian motifs, including grape clusters, pelicans, and ducks, as well as fantastical winged lions.

1027 Flatbush Avenue, Brooklyn · 1929

KINGS THEATRE
(ORIGINALLY LOEW'S KINGS THEATRE)
RAPP & RAPP, ARCHITECTS
Opened in 1929 as a movie palace designed by the show-biz architectural firm of Rapp & Rapp at 1027 Flatbush Avenue, the Loew's Kings Theatre (now the Kings Theatre) features one of the most opulent interiors (not shown) in the city. A marvelous orange mural against a black background in terracotta represents the movies with showy peacocks and a jester's face, surrounded by sinuous vines.

STERLING BOWLING AND BILLIARD ACADEMY
ISAAC KALLICH, ARCHITECT
This small-scale polychrome terracotta gem at the intersection of Nostrand Avenue and Sterling Place in the
North Crown Heights section of Brooklyn was originally built by Russian émigré architect Isaac Kallich as the Sterling
Bowling and Billiard Academy in 1929. The ornamentation, which could be called Baroque or Neoclassical Deco,
has nothing to do with bowling or billiards.

1 East 65ᵗʰ Street · 1929

TEMPLE EMANU-EL
ROBERT D. KOHN, CHARLES BUTLER, AND CLARENCE STEIN,
IN ASSOCIATION WITH MAYERS, MURRAY & PHILLIP, ARCHITECTS
One of the largest synagogues in the world, Temple Emanu-El, was designed on
the site of the former Mrs. William B. Astor House in a mixture of styles, incorporating elements of
Romanesque Revival and Moorish Revival, while offering fantastical Art Deco detailing. Since Jewish law prohibits representation of the human
figure, the temple is bedecked with two-dimensionally stylized, Deco-esque images of the twelve tribes of Israel:
the lion for Judah, and the coild snake for Dan (following pages).

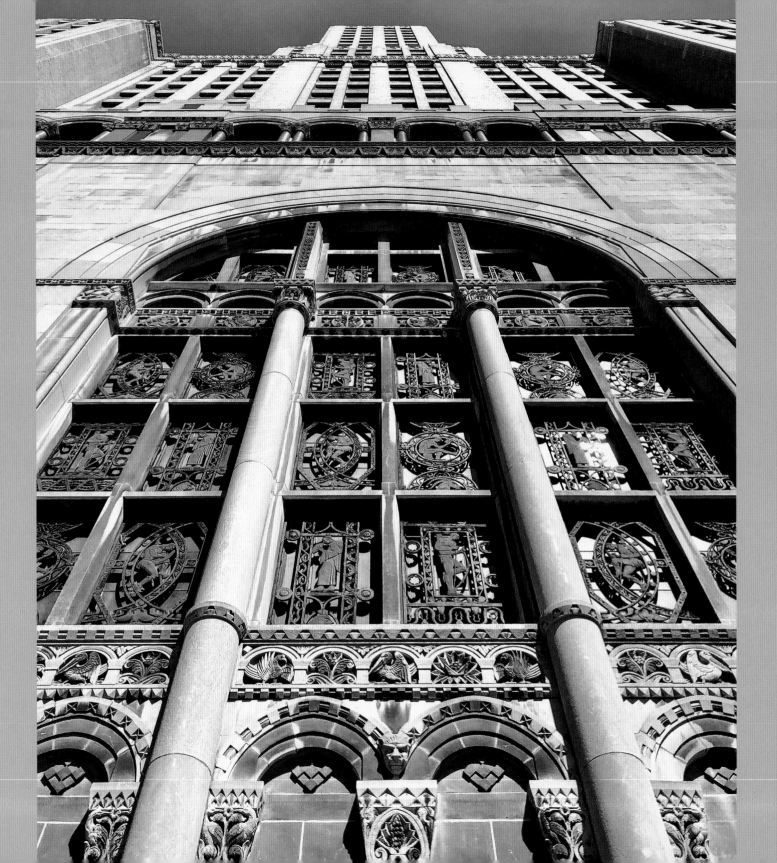

(FORMERLY WILLIAMSBURGH SAVINGS BANK TOWER)
HALSEY, MCCORMACK & HELMER, ARCHITECTS

The Deco facade of the former Williamsburgh Savings Bank Tower in downtown Brooklyn is chockful of symbols of the advantages of thrift. An arched, carved limestone frieze features a pineapple (a symbol of welcome); next to a stork (parenthood); a floral motif; a pelican (a symbol of motherhood and sacrifice, said to pierce its breast with its beak to provide blood to nurture its young); and a fern motif. Owls on the facade represent the wisdom of saving.

The slender-towered skyscraper bank is designed in a synthesis of Art Deco and Romanesque Byzantine styles. The 128-foot-long, 72-foot-wide, 63-foot-high banking chamber (not shown) features a barrel-vaulted gold mosaic ceiling, and a Cosmatesque floor is set in twenty-two different kinds of marble, to bedazzle the customers.

CHRYSLER BUILDING
WILLIAM VAN ALEN, ARCHITECT

Fearsome eagle's heads forged in the new amalgam of "Nirosta" steel jut out like Machine Age gargoyles from the corner setbacks below the arched spire of the Chrysler Building, built by William Van Alen in 1930. In a style that could be called Hubcap Modern, winged urns evocative of the radiator cap of a 1929 Chrysler automobile make the building a thousand-foot-tall corporate billboard. During the Depression, the ground floor housed a showroom for new Chryslers. Triangular windows (page 115) in the crown of the Chrysler Building glow like Dan Flavin sculptures on the Midtown skyline at dusk. The faceted glass panel above the Chrysler entrance could have been taken straight from a German Expressionist film like Fritz Lang's *Metropolis* (1927). Lang said he was inspired to make *Metropolis* after seeing the lit-up Manhattan skyline for the first time from an ocean liner.

ST. BARTHOLOMEW'S EPISCOPAL CHURCH
BERTRAM GOODHUE, ARCHITECT
HILDRETH MEIÈRE, MOSAICS
LEE LAWRIE, SCULPTURE

Extraordinary mosaics by Hildreth Meière enliven the St. Bartholomew's Episcopal Church interior (opposite, above, and following pages, right),
with the birds of the air and the fish of the sea playing prominent roles. Meanwhile masterful sculpture work by Lee Lawrie complements this
decorative Deco aviary, offering here (following pages, left) a stalwart, sharply defined eagle.

(FORMERLY CITY BANK–FARMERS TRUST COMPANY BUILDING)
CROSS & CROSS, ARCHITECTS

Twenty Exchange Place (formerly the Citibank–Farmers Trust Building), sheathed in Alabama Rookwood limestone with a
Mohegan granite base, was, when built, the tallest stone-clad building in the world, at fifty-seven stories and a skosh over 685 feet tall.
A pediment of a bison head, symbolic of the Farmers Trust's agricultural interests, is flanked by two coiled snakes.
A lunette is adorned by a spread mosaic American spread eagle against a diapered pattern (following pages). Especially during
the Great Depression, banks wanted to identify with the solidity of the Federal government.

21 West Street · 1931

STARRETT & VAN VLECK, ARCHITECTS
Designed by Goldwin Starrett and Ernest Alan Van Vleck in 1931, 21 West Street is a thirty-one story Art Deco
apartment building with finely detailed brickwork suggestive of woven fabric and lavish architectural finishes.
It is marked on its exterior by a series of setbacks which taper at the top floors, offering very much a Jazz-Age feel.

JACOB M. FELSON, ARCHITECT

This nineteen-story apartment building by Jacob M. Felson, best known for his geometric Deco apartments that line the Grand Concourse in the Bronx, features plant motifs in delicate terracotta shades of celadon, viridian, emerald, ochre, cream, and violet.

THE CRANLYN APARTMENTS
H. FELDMAN, ARCHITECT

Magnificent mustard-colored peacocks (above) with geometrically stylized chevron tails against a black background are paired off in this eye-catching polychromatic terracotta panel above an exterior doorway. The Jazz Age brickwork facade of this small-scale apartment building in tree-lined Brooklyn Heights features a Deco arabesque fantasia in bronze (opposite) in front of the lobby desk.

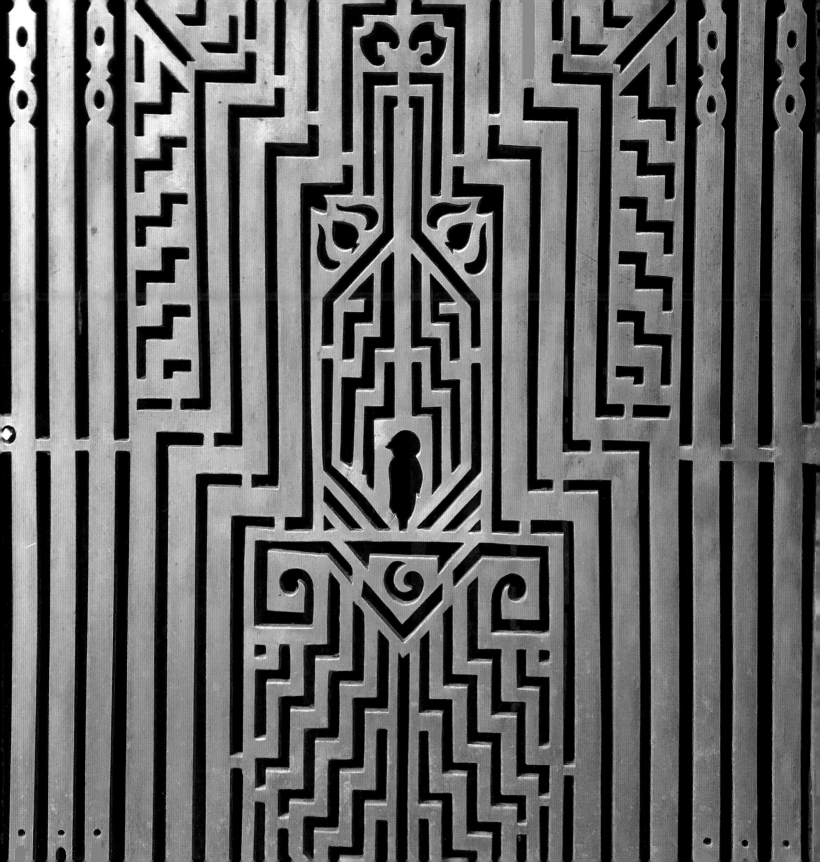

SHREVE, LAMB & HARMON, ARCHITECTS
The fifty-eight story Fifth Avenue Art Deco tower by Shreve, Lamb & Harmon was considered a thoroughly
"modern architectural treatment" at the time and meant as an honest expression
reflecting the needs of an up-to-date office building. An architect's muse (opposite) in Classical garb cradles a spread eagle in her right hand and
a maquette of the skysraper itself in her left. Gold concrete fronds (above) reflect the setback style.

MILLAN HOUSE
ANDREW J. THOMAS, ARCHITECT

Millan House is an eleven-story apartment house designed in 1931 by architect Andrew J. Thomas that is particularly notable for its bestiary of limestone-carved animals, including jowly bulldogs, Aztec-feathered parrots, lapdogs, and bunnies to celebrate domesticity, and ornate wildlife symbolizing the great outdoors—owls' heads, pelicans, great cats, and possums to name only a few (opposite). A humorous, spread-eagled bat gazes down with a simian grin from his cornice perch (above). Art Deco stripped down the plastic treatment of the entire facade seen in Art Nouveau, and placed ornament where it was most visible—at the cornices, setbacks, upon column capitals, and embedded within door surrounds, as evident here.

EL DORADO
EMERY ROTH AND MARGON & HOLDER, ARCHITECTS
The twin-towered El Dorado at 300 Central Park West, one of the most prestigious addresses on
the park, was designed in 1931 by Margon & Holder with the firm's associate architect Emery Roth,
who specialized in luxury apartment buildings. The entryway features chamfered corners (a frequent Deco motif),
and a bronze panel decorated with stylized ferns and bouquets of flowers.

EMPIRE STATE BUILDING
SHREVE, LAMB & HARMON, ARCHITECTS
A modern marvel at the time of its construction, New York's most famous Art Deco tower—and perhaps
still its most famous building—needs no introduction. Officially 102 stories tall, at the time of its construction it was
the world's tallest building and, with its shining steel construction, was a dazzling expression of the age. German Expressionist eagles cut in
limestone surmout attached pillars, adding drama to the entranceway (above). A flamelike, organiform metal disk on the marble lobby wall
commemorates the skysraper's swift completion (following pages).

MARCH · 17 · 1930 MARCH · 1 · 1931

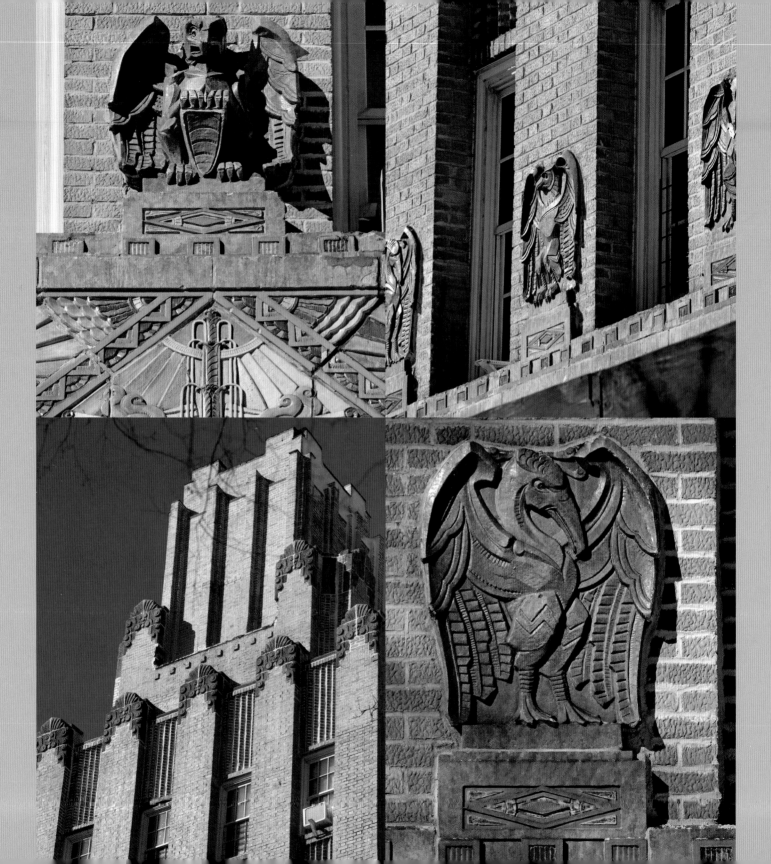

PARK PLAZA APARTMENTS
HORACE GINSBERG AND MARVIN FINE, ARCHITECTS
The Park Plaza Apartments, completed by Horace Ginsberg and Marvin Fine in 1931, were among the
earliest Deco apartments in the staid Bronx. The jewel in the crown of the Park Plaza are eight brightly
colored terracotta spandrels. A row of American eagles (opposite, top) in bronze-colored terracotta protect the
piers of an apartment building above a parti-colored beltline. Traditionally, pelicans (above) are symbols of motherly love and
self-sacrifice, based on the myth that they pierce their own breasts with their beaks to provide life-giving blood to their brood. A zigzag frieze
presents repeating images of the tower itself as the crown of the city, against the radiant rays of the rising sun—a motif dating back to medieval
Germany.

1619 Boston Road, Bronx · 1931

HERMAN RIDDER JUNIOR HIGH SCHOOL
WALTER C. MARTIN, ARCHITECT

A realization of then–superintendent of school building Walter C. Martin's intention in 1929 to build New York's "first thoroughly modernistic school building,"
the Herman Ridder Junior High School is a wonder. Designed by Walter C. Martin in 1931 with bas-relief designs, heroic-size maidens holding books,
and a crowning Babylonian ziggurat-like tower top, the building is a triumph of the Deco style in stone.

114

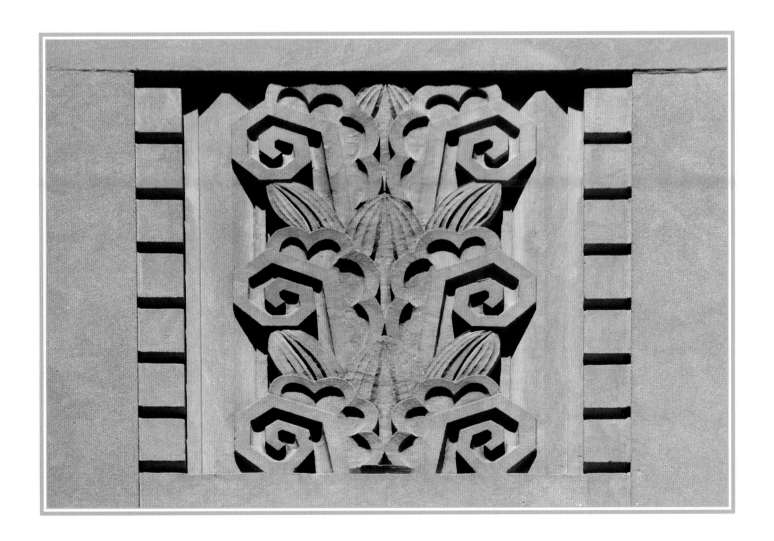

WALDORF ASTORIA
SCHULTZE & WEAVER, ARCHITECTS
The legendary Waldorf Astoria, designed by Schultze & Weaver, for decades stood as the epitome in luxury hotels. Upon its completion
the world's tallest hotel (at forty-seven stories), it has long been an icon of glamour and still stands as an expression of the exuberance that
characterized the Deco age. Elaborate vines, flowers, and ferns adorn this Neoclassically inspired Art Deco metal sculptural grille (opposite),
accompanied by a grace figure with long tresses and a pleated skirt. A deeply cut limeston haut relief of sharply angled ferns framed by square
dentiles are indicative of the Waldorf's Neoclassical-Deco fusion.

117

70 Pine Street · 1932

CLINTON & RUSSELL, HOLTON & GEORGE, ARCHITECTS
Formerly known as the Cities Service Building and the American International Building, 70 Pine Street
was designed by Clinton & Russell, Holton & George in the Art Deco style for Cities Service Company (later Citgo).
Cliff Parkhurst designed the aluminum ornamentation, which includes reliefs above each set of entrance doors, spandrels with
sharp arrises above the lower-story windows, and a ventilation grille (not shown) on Cedar Street.

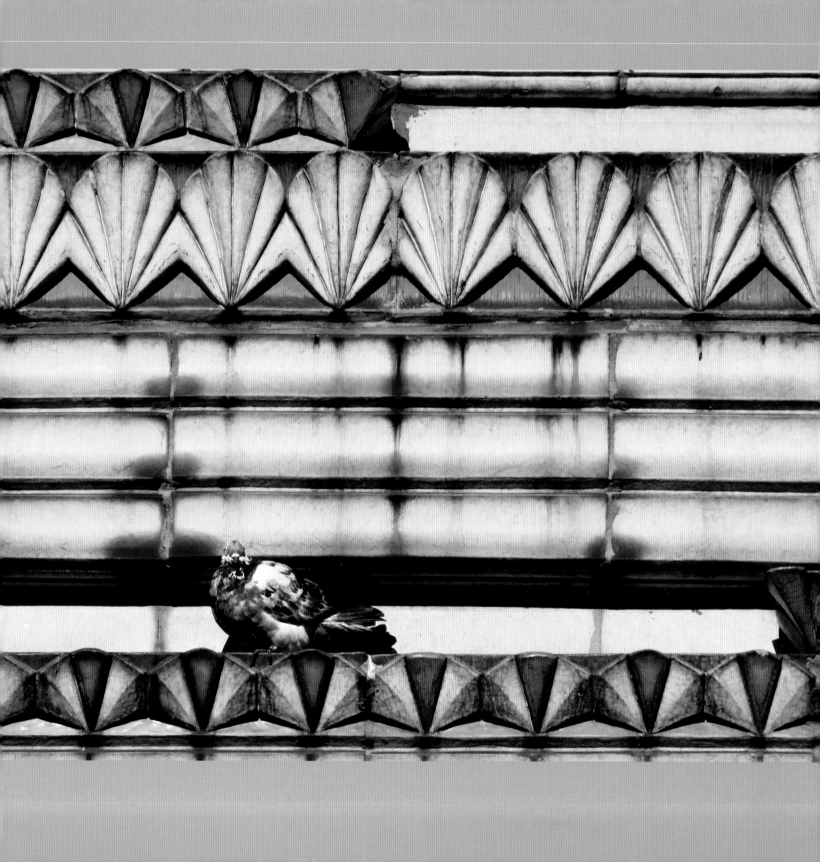

MORRIS BERNARD ADLER, ARCHITECT
This brick and terracotta eye catcher in the Bedford Stuyvesant section of
Brooklyn was designed by Morris Bernard Adler. Though in poor repair, the building retains an air of its
former ebullience in these highly embellished, geometric, polychromatic fan and fern shapes. Linear design, meant to be scanned across the
surface to add a visual sensation of zip and motion, along with serial pattern repetition, are hallmarks of Art Deco.

125 Barclay Street · 1932

WORLD TELEGRAM BUILDING
HOWELL & THOMAS, ARCHITECTS
Built in 1932, 125 Barclay Street is an example of the evolution of Art Deco into Streamline Moderne and
Neoclassical styles, with simplified motifs of waveform lines and copper-colored rosettes. Streamlined, copper-colored
sunflower heads (above) owe more to Neoclassical motifs than Art Deco. Minimal ornamentation of a green stringcourse and
lintels above the windows on the upper floors (opposite) are typical of cost-conscious Streamline Moderne.

AMBASSADOR APARTMENTS
LUCIAN PISCIOTTA, ARCHITECT
The Ambassador, in St. George, Staten Island, was designed by Lucian Pisciotta in 1932 and features frond patterns in
white, cream, and blue terracotta alongside an abstract pattern of chevrons and leaves in tawny orange, blue, gold, and indigo.
The name *AMBASSADOR* is emblazoned in a Deco font above the entranceway (oppositie and following pages), flanked by Chambellan-esque
curling ferns and surmounted by Edgar Brandt–inspired frozen fountains in blue and gold. The architect, Lucian Pisciotta,
specialized in luxury apartment buildings.

32 Avenue of the Americas · 1932

AT&T LONG DISTANCE BUILDING
RALPH WALKER, ARCHITECT
HILDRETH MEIÈRE, LOBBY MOSAIC DECOR

Mosaic of a kangaroo, a peasant woman, and a lamb represent the antipodes (above) in the trip around the AT&T Building's ceiling, connected by the golden thread of communication. A sinuous Chinese tiger bows down to an elegant Mandarin in a headdress and silk gown, reclining before Chinese pagodas (opposite, top). A bare-breasted Egyptian noblewoman reclines on her barge on the Nile, accompanied by a pair of Nubian cubs, while passing the pyramids (following pages).

159

BRONX COUNTY COURTHOUSE
MAX HAUSEL AND JOSEPH H. FREEDLANDER, ARCHITECTS
American eagles emblazon the gilded bronze gate of the Neoclassical Deco Bronx County Courthouse at
851 Grand Concourse, proudly symbolizing the fortitude of the U.S. Justice system. Neoclassicism, always thought
appropriate for government buildings, made a resurgence during the Depression because of the style's relative simplicity.
A polychromatic bronze screen (opposite) features spead-winged eagles and winged hourglasses in the style of ancient Rome to portray the
inevitable march of justice.

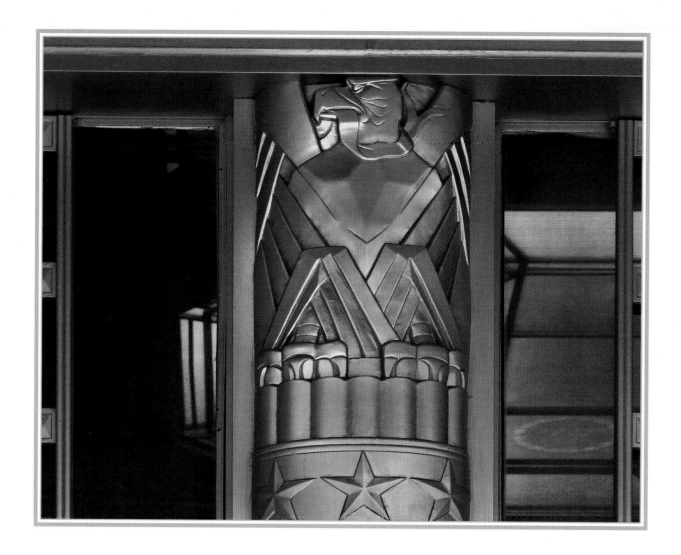

CROSS & CROSS AND PENNINGTON, LEWIS & MILLS, ARCHITECTS

U.S. Post Offices, like this Depression-era one at 90 Church Street, often feature images of strength, reliability, and celerity. The mail will get through! Symbolizing the strength and unity of the Federal government, a resolute Deco American eagle surmounts a star-spangled bundle of fasces (above). Built in the depths of the Great Depression by Cross & Cross in 1933, the post office building combines Neoclassical, Art Deco, and Streamline Moderne styles. There were similarities between Streamline Moderne and Fascist decorative artwork during the 1930s. This fierce American eagle (opposite), guarding a fasces and vertical stars and stripes, is especially striking because of its corner location.

Rainey Memorial Gates, Bronx Zoo · 1934

PAUL MANSHIP, SCULPTOR

A verdigris Deco menagerie tops the double-arched gates of the Bronx Zoo by premier Deco artist Paul Manship. The animals here seem to reside in their natural habitats, a gem of small-scale grouping. The close observer is rewarded with glimpses of owls, fawn, and harts in their stylized habitat, with even a reigning baboon!

125 Worth Street · 1935

(FORMERLY NYC DEPARTMENT OF HEALTH BUILDING)
CHARLES B. MEYERS, ARCHITECT
OSCAR BACH, METALWORK

Also known as the New York City Health Building, 125 Worth Street was designed by Charles B. Meyers and completed in 1935. The front and side entrances have bronze grillwork and other metal design, including medallions with health themes (not shown). A Deco-esque statue of a weathered-green metal American eagle with upraised wings atop a limestone column guards the entrance (opposite). A cornice of nearly 3-D chow dog heads and an anthemium is a purely Neoclassical overlay below a Deco-influenced beltcourse of winged roundels in bas relief.

SALVATION ARMY HEADQUARTERS
RALPH WALKER, ARCHITECT

The Salvation Army Headquarters was designed in a monumental, clean-lined Deco style by Ralph Walker of Voorhees,
Gmelin & Walker in 1935 and clad in brick with cast stone ornament near the top and around the
distinctive recessed entry portal. This metalwork eagle (above) speaks to the Salvation Army's determination and fortitude,
with the classic ornament symbolizing new beginnings, resilience, and stamina in face of difficulty. Curtain folds in limestone form a mysterious
grotto beyond the pedestrian way, secured by bronze gates in abstract Deco patterns.

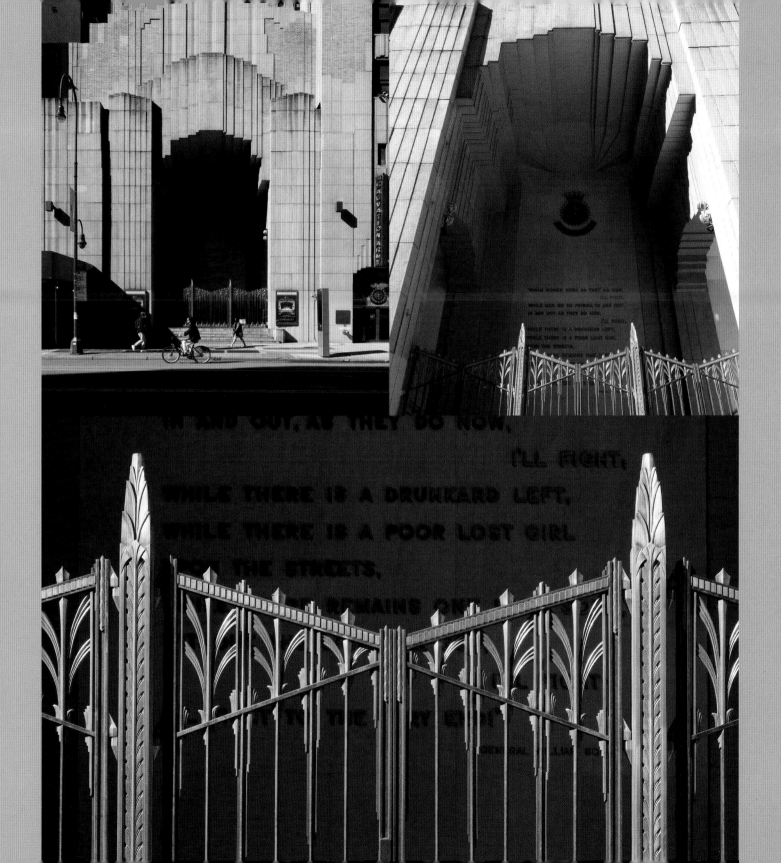

750 Grand Concourse, Bronx · 1937

JACOB M. FELSON, ARCHITECT

Part of the Grand Concourse Historic District, 750 Grand Concourse, designed by Jacob M. Felson, exudes a kind of Hollywood grandeur. Here the lobby (opposite) suggests nothing so much as a ballroom to host the likes of Ginger Rogers and Fred Astaire. Gilded circular bands in the ceiling and walls are reflected in the terrazzo floor, suggesting music and movement—very much at the heart of the Jazz Age. Architects hoped to lure increasingly wealthy Manhattanites "uptown" to the Grand Concourse (twice as wide as the Champs-Élysées!) with the dernier crí in Deco design.

FISH BUILDING
HORACE GINSBERN AND MARVIN FINE, ARCHITECTS
A fantastically colorful mosaic mural featuring bright sunfish, grumpy grouper, amoebae, and sea plants lines the
entranceway of this apartment building on the Grand Concourse. The mural is pure Deco, while the rounded corners are
Streamline Moderne. Amazing attention was given to the undersea mosaic scene's coloration, pattern, and detailing. It is unclear
why a marine design appears on the Grand Concourse, other than for the sheer exuberance of the craftsmanship.

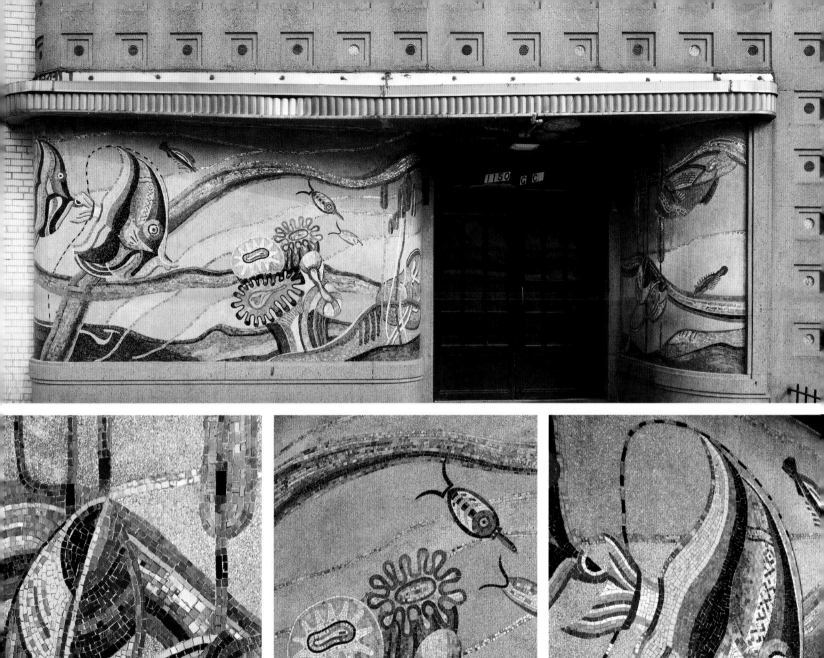

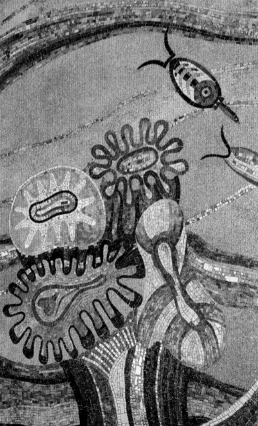

1166 Grand Concourse, Bronx · 1938

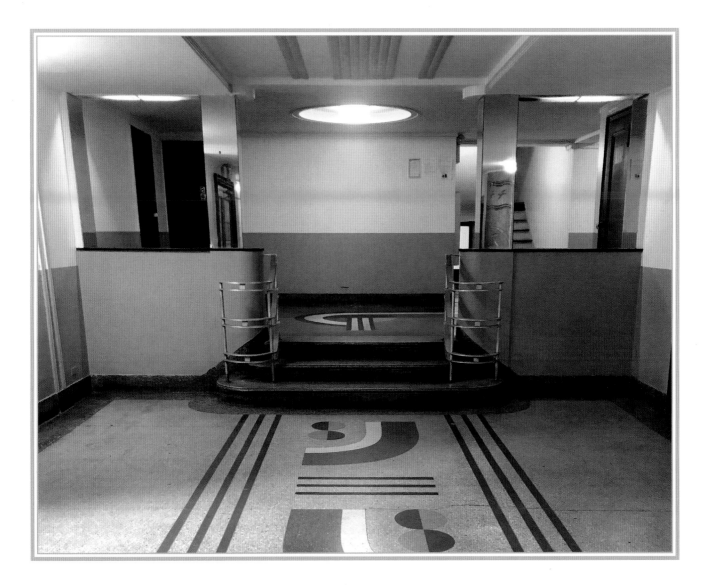

JACOB M. FELSON, ARCHITECT
Another gem in the Art Deco enclave along the Grand Concourse in the Bronx is number 1166. Attention
to detail is evident in the extraordinary mosaics that effortlessly coordinate elements of sea, land, and air.
Here and within, the serious geometric side of the style is leavened with lighthearted touches.
The pure geometry of the central lobby is a stark, no-frills version of Depression Moderne design (above); so the building makes an interesting
transition, spanning both schools of design in the late 1930s.

ASSOCIATED ARCHITECTS; RAYMOND HOOD, LEAD ARCHITECT

An ensemble of forms, Rockefeller Center showcases a magnificent array of Art Deco details. A gilded cast bronze bas-relief by Alfred Janniot of 1934, titled *Friendship Between America and France* (above and following pages, right, in detail), signifies, well, just that—two heroically scaled allegorical women meeting mid-ocean. The following pages offer a treasury of decorative expression. A seagull with russet and limestone-colored wings (following page, left); the gilding and polychrome was embellished by architectural colorist Leon V. Solon. A beatific Saint Francis (page 182), patron saint of animals, features a gilded halo of doves in this polychrome limestone intaglio by Lee Lawrie. A finny-footed Nereid (page 183, left), by sculptor René Paul Chambellan, in cast bronze with flowing Deco hair strides a fantasy fountainhead sea creature. This large-scale, sculptural grille (page 183, top right) in carved limestone, gilding, and polychrome from 1937 is one of fifteen panels, or "hieroglyphs," by noted architectural sculptor Lee Lawrie, representing "The Story of Mankind." Lawrie's intaglio relief set in limestone from 1933 shows three gilded passant-gardant lions (page 183, bottom right) that have been incorporated in the arms of British sovereigns since the time of Richard I. They surmount a row of red and gilded Tudor roses, another symbol of British royalty. The immortal, winged horse Pegasus (page 184), usually depicted in pure white, is associated with creativity and inspiration in Greek mythology, and symbolizes the cultural exchange of Franco-American relations. A Leda figure rides a swan's back (page 185).

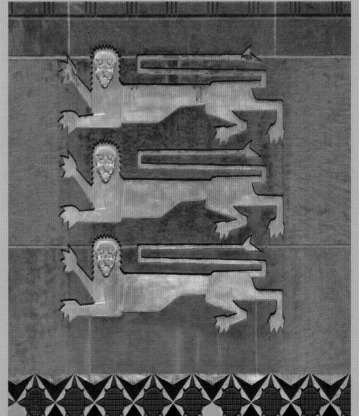

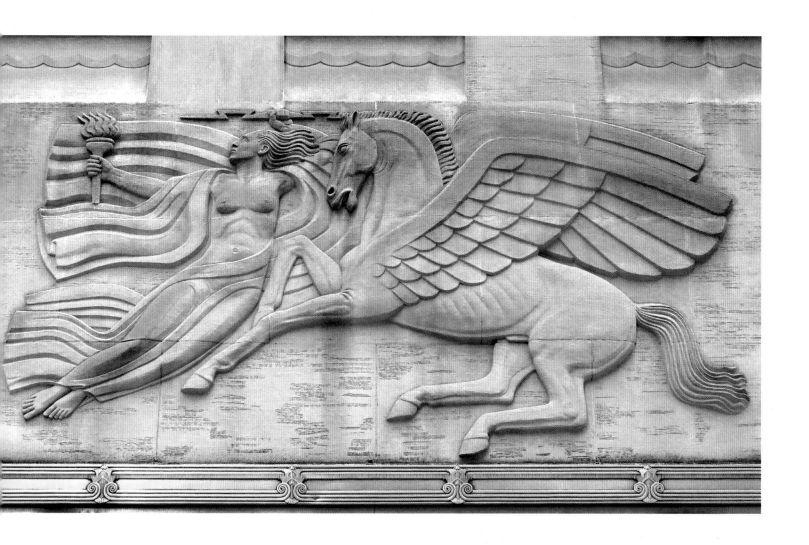

10 Grand Army Plaza, Brooklyn · 1941

BROOKLYN PUBLIC LIBRARY
RAYMOND F. ALMIRALL AND ALFRED M. GITHENS & FRANCIS KELLY, ARCHITECTS
THOMAS HUDSON JONES, SCULPTOR

The starkly streamlined limestone-clad Beaux-Arts facade of the Brooklyn Public Library's central branch off Grand Army Plaza
was built by architects Alfred Morton Githens and Francis Kelly in 1941, a late example of the style. An iron screen above the
entranceway features gilded figures by Deco sculptor Thomas Hudson Jones, representing the evolution of art and science as well as famous
tales from litereature: Paul Bunyan's ox, Babe the Blue Ox; Moby Dick; The Scarlet Letter; Tom Sawyer; a bust of Walt Whitman; and even Brer
Rabbit and the Tar Baby (still considered part of the canon in 1940).

T·H·JONES

BROOKLYN PUBLIC LIBRARY

SQUIRE VICKERS, HEINS & LA FARGE, AND JOHN H. PERRY

Deco and Deco-esque details are to be found below the city, as well as above. The 33rd Street subway station eagle in tile (above), by the Grueby Faience Company, was designed by John H. Perry. Horns of plenty hold the 137th Street Station sign (opposite, top), designed by Heins & La Farge and manufactured by the Atlantic Terra Cotta Company; dating from 1904, this feature perhaps anticipates Art Deco, in its coloration and zigzag number-framing lines. This subway sign (opposite, bottom left and middle) is a Beaux-Arts overlay of a Deco-style seahorse, in keeping with the overall decorative program of the Graybar Building's interior; the seahorse features marvelously sculpted bronze fins, scales, and coiled tale, over a rondel of rolling waves. This 125th Street station mosaic (opposite, bottom right) dates from the station's opening in 1925 and was made by the Atlantic Terra Cotta Company in partnership with the Manhattan Glass Tile Company; the design is by Squire Vickers.

To Kaarina and Platypus. Thankful to have been able to explore and document New York City's Art Deco treasures during the height of lockdown.

—A. G.